BUILDING FAMILIES

BUILDING FAMILIES

Breaking Ungodly Influences, Lifestyles and Desires while Influencing the Next Generation

CLARENCE V. RUSSELL III

Suffolk, Virginia

BUILDING FAMILIES:
Breaking Ungodly Influences, Lifestyles and Desires while Influencing the Next Generation

Copyright © 2020 by Clarence V. Russell III
All rights reserved.

All rights reserved. This book is protected by the copyright laws of the United States of America. This book may not be copied or reprinted for commercial gain or profit. The use of quotations or occasional page copying for personal or group study is permitted and encouraged. Permission will be granted upon request.

Final Step Publishing, LLC

PO Box 1441
Suffolk, VA 23439

Soft cover ISBN: 978-1-7355280-2-1

For Worldwide Distribution. Printed in U.S.A.

DEDICATION

This book is dedicated to my family whom I stand for,

my wife Jaimi and my children Clarence IV, Caitlyn, Casey and Caleb.

Also to the family that I have been called to lead, St. Paul Baptist Church.

Most of all to the God who loved me enough to send His son to come and stand for me.

CONTENTS

Introduction   8

CHAPTER 1
Let's Get Real   13

CHAPTER 2
Dealing with Daddy's Devils   29

CHAPTER 3
How to Stand for the House   45

CHAPTER 4
Maintain Your Profession   53

CHAPTER 5
Manipulate Your Perspective   63

CHAPTER 6
Mastering the Process   79

Author's Bio   87

INTRODUCTION

    I recently changed primary care physicians. In preparation for my annual physical, I was required to arrive at the doctor's office thirty minutes ahead of my appointment time. Upon arriving, I was required to fill out several forms. One form was for my personal information and another was about my medical history. The third form was an extensive section on my family's medical history. I am sure that anyone that has undergone this process is familiar with this line of questioning. As I began to reflect on previous medical experiences, I recalled that every time that I went to a new doctor or even had a physical, I was asked the same questions. These questions were necessary to determine what illnesses or diseases that I may be at a higher risk for contracting. This process started me thinking about all of the negativity that we inherit. The questions asked by medical professionals search for our biological inheritance, however, we also inherit things spiritually.

    The Bible is full of examples of inherited traits both negative and positive. Some of the effects of negativity being handed down through generations can be seen through scriptures such as Exodus 20:5-6. It reads, "Thou shalt not bow down thyself to them, or serve them; for I, the Lord thy God, am a jealous God, visiting the iniquity of the father upon the children unto the third and fourth generation of them that hate me; And showing mercy unto thousands." This pericope of scripture gives a clear example of how bad things can impact several generations. One of the major examples of this issue sets the tone for the Bible itself. The sin of Adam doesn't just end with him but all of man is contaminated with sin as a result. The apostle Paul confirms this in Romans 5:17, "For if by one man's offense death reigned by one, much more they who receive abundance of grace and of the gift of righteousness shall reign in life by one, Jesus Christ." Paul says that as a result of one man's offense or wrongdoing death began to reign over mankind. This one man that Paul is referring to is Adam. Whether it is through biblical study or through personal experience, most people have discovered that bad things can be passed down. Even though this is an aspect of reality that we must deal with I don't believe that it is the will of God for our lives.

The other side of the coin speaks to the positive traits that are inherited through family. The Bible is full of accounts regarding the generational transfer of blessings. While reading the book of Genesis, the blessing of Abraham can be seen being passed down through several generations. It was passed from Abraham to his son Isaac and from Isaac to his son Jacob. As a matter of fact, as believers we are considered the seed of

Abraham through faith. The apostle Paul clearly states this fact in Romans 4:16. It reads, "Therefore it is of faith, that it might be by grace; to the end the promise might be sure to all the seed; not to that only which is of the law, but to that also which is of the faith of Abraham; who is the father of us all." This connection gives us access to the promise that God made to Abraham in Genesis. Galatians 4:28 says, "Now we, brethren, as Isaac was, are the children of promise." If this example is not enough to establish the fact that blessings also flow through families then the next passage of scripture, which serves as the foundation for this book, should provide the needed clarity. In Joshua 24, the children of Israel have inherited the blessing of the promised land that was promised to their forefathers and Abraham. They are walking in the blessing that was handed down through the previous generations.

Joshua understands that both the positive and negative can be handed down through family. However, it comes down to a choice made by the individual to determine what will be accepted and what will be rejected. We will begin our examination at verse 14 that says: "Now therefore fear the Lord, and serve him in sincerity and in truth: and put away the gods which your fathers served on the other side of the river, and in Egypt; and serve ye the Lord."

And Joshua 24:15, "And if it seems evil unto you to serve the Lord, choose you this day whom ye will serve; whether the gods which your fathers served that were on the other side of the river, or the gods of the Amorites, in whose land ye dwell: but as for me and my house, we will serve the Lord."

This book is entitled *Building Families*. *Building* is an acronym for Breaking Ungodly Influences, Lifestyles and Desires while Inspiring the Next Generation. Together we will execute an exegetical approach to this passage of scripture. In doing so we will uncover the choices, charges, and challenges that Joshua identifies as the necessary components for building a godly family. Let's begin the journey!

chapter 1

LET'S GET REAL

Our foundation for this journey can be found in Joshua 24:14-15. It states, "Now therefore fear the Lord, and serve him in sincerity and in truth: and put away the gods which your fathers served on the other side of the flood, and in Egypt; and serve ye the Lord. And if it seem evil unto you to serve the Lord, choose you this day whom ye will serve; whether the gods which your fathers served that were on the other side of the flood, or the gods of the Amorites, in whose land ye dwell: but as for me and my house, we will serve the Lord."

The story is familiar to us in the church as believers. We see Joshua confronting the children of Israel asking them what they're going to do. He asks are you going to serve the Lord or are you going to mimic and imitate? He's asking whether they will pick up the same habits and do the same things that they've seen done previously. Now, this question seems to be one that all of us have to answer at some juncture in our lives: are you going to serve the Lord or not?

Seems simple enough. Everybody who has given their life to Christ has made that decision or been confronted with it and wrestled with that choice at some point or another in their life. But the thing that makes Joshua's demanding inquiry stand out is the fact that he asked the question *after* the Israelites already made it to the Promised Land.

He's not asking them this as they are preparing to inherit what God has promised them. They have already received God's blessings and occupied the land. Their wandering is over. They've been through the deliverance. They've endured the process, the wilderness phase. Now they are in the promised place.

A lot of us are still on our way to our promise— the manifestation of the thing that we're believing in God for. We are on our way to it; *they* have it. They are living in it.

And then Joshua asked them, "What are going to do?" Well, Joshua, from a lot of what we know, tells us there are some things that we have to do in order to get to the promise. So, it would seem to me that because of where we are in this text, that these people have already made the decision to serve the Lord.

There's a whole generation of people that have died out in the wilderness. They've seen their parents and grandparents drop dead because they did not believe the words that that the Lord gave Moses. So, it seems that this is a different generation of followers. This is a generation that has seen the penalty for not believing and trusting God, so that question would seem redundant, but Joshua understood that a lot of times, we act like we are 'all in' for the plan of God, just to get what we want from him.

And for that reason, many of us struggle with spiritual delivery because we only do what it takes to get what we want from God. We say, "God, I want you to fix this, I want you to turn this around. So, I'm going to be faithful until you do it. I'm going to be committed until you do it."

It seems funny how we forget the context of this biblical story because you have to understand that Joshua is a little bit older than the people that he's leading. Yes, Joshua and Caleb were of the generation that died out. Now, if you go back a couple chapters in the book of Joshua, it lets you know that Caleb at this point was about 84 years old.

And he declares that he's just as strong now at 84 as he was at 44 when God made him the promise. So, you have to figure out that Joshua is close to around the same age. Joshua remembers how the children of Israel prayed to be delivered from Egypt. Joshua remembers their history and recognizes where they're coming from. He knew how they prayed for a deliverer. And once the deliverer came and brought them across the miles and brought them out of Egypt, they arrived to the Red Sea and started complaining.

> *Every trial should not have to redefine your relationship with God if you say you are who you are.*

The Lord moved again. They crossed the Red Sea. Three days later, they were thirsty and started complaining again. Joshua said, "I recognize that now that we're in the promise, it's only going to be a matter of time before something else frustrates these people."

You need to anticipate that something is going to frustrate you tomorrow. Something is going to frustrate you a week from now. Something is going to get on your nerves again. And God should not have to be put to the test every time somebody gets on your nerves.

Every trial should not have to redefine your relationship with God if you say you are who you are. The message here is: Oh, hush with your whining. You ought to know who I am by now. All this stuff we've been through... why has there have to be an ultimatum every time you encounter a trial or you have a test? When are you going to learn to grow up, stand up, and walk in my steps and statutes and precepts? Why do you need a miracle every time you stamp your toe? Some stuff you just have to learn how to deal with, so Joshua said, "Yes, we are in the promise. But I still need to know what you're going to do." And, so, he begins to give them some instructions before he asked the question. I want to ask you the same question: what are you going to do? Because it's time to get real. It's time for us to be as serious about our commitment to God as we want God to be about his commitment to us. Your thought cannot be, *Oh God you know I'm just so faithful* simply because you need something.

But when that need is met where are you going to be? That's why some of us can't come out of the mess that we're in. You need a little drama to keep you praying. You need a little turmoil or some issues that keep you committed.

I know you're thinking *there isn't any preacher who is going to tell me that,* especially in a book. But the Lord isn't bringing you out of all the stuff that you're in because he knows that once you come all the way out, you're gone.

If you really want to know how somebody feels about you, wait until they don't need you. For example, your girlfriend or boyfriend may not have a vehicle and so they call on you to take them places. Wait until she or he gets their own car and no longer needs you to drive them anywhere. If they continue to call you every day after *that,* you may have something real.

You don't hear a lot of people talking about the fear of the Lord anymore. Let's look at what Joshua says at Verse 14: "Now therefore, Fear the Lord." The first thing Joshua tells them to do is fear the Lord. This is not 2 Timothy 1:7 where it says that God has not given us the spirit of fear. This is not a reference to the spirit of fear. Here, fear the Lord does not mean to be afraid of God. But the fear of the Lord means that there ought to be a reverential trust there.

> *It is His desire that I fear him—that there's a certain amount of reverence that I just have for who God is.*

Many people do not fear the Lord anymore. What they have is the fear of hell. Some of us grew up believing that everything we did wrong was going to see us to hell. We weren't taught that once you gave your life to Christ, hell is no longer an option for you. The fear of hell is not God's intent. It is His desire that I fear him—that there's a certain amount of reverence that I just have for who God is. The fear of the Lord is something that God puts in us.

The fear of the Lord makes you act differently. Jeremiah 32:40 says, "and I will make an everlasting covenant with them. Then I will not turn away from doing them good, but I will put my fear in their hearts that they shall not depart from me."

Do you see that? In the above verse, God tells Jeremiah that he is going to give you this fear, but in 2 Timothy 1:7, Paul tells us that God did not give us the *spirit* of fear. The fear of the Lord, as in "when I put my fear in their hearts, they shall not depart from me" is going to cause you to think a certain way towards him. It's going to cause you to act a certain way; it's going to dictate some parameters of your relationship with God. The fear of the Lord is going to do three things: it's going to cause you to respect his position; it's going to cause you to see the relevance of his plan; and it's going to cause you to rely on his provision.

Now, let's consider the first thing: it will cause you to respect his position. Psalm 19:7-9 says,

> The law of the Lord is pretty perfect. Converting the soul, the testimony of the Lord is sure, making the simple, the statues of the Lord are right, rejoicing the heart, the commandment of the Lord is pure, and enlightening the eyes, the fear of the Lord is clean, enduring forever. The ordinances of the Lord are true and righteous all together.

What David is talking about here is the law and the precepts and the way of God. First of all, the fear of the Lord will teach you to respect God's position. You need to understand how God feels about certain things because if we're going to serve Him then we have to be on His side, and we have to know how He feels about various issues.

Were you looking at it like that? Many folks rely too much on what they feel—they try to feel their way in line with God. Well, that doesn't sit well with me. How does God feel about it? Then that's going to tell you how you need to sit with it.

The text says, "...the fear of the Lord is clean, enduring forever." You need to understand that your perception of stuff may not be clean and is tainted based upon the potential for personal gain, how you feel, and your perception. Many things are tainted because we look at them through the lens of how it's going to benefit us.

In Ezekiel 44:23, the Lord says that He has a responsibility. It says, "...and they shall teach my people the difference between the holy and common and cause them to discern between unclean and the clean." The way that you're able to distinguish what's right from what's wrong, what's holy or unholy, or what's clean or unclean, is by recognizing where God stands on the issue. It is not based on what we used to do.

Remember, Joshua is sitting in the tent telling these folks, "Look, you can't go and mimic what you've seen done."

So, what are *you* going to do? You're going to fear the Lord; you're going to serve Him in sincerity and in truth, and you're going to put away the gods of your fathers. We will get to the gods of the fathers shortly.

We need to figure out and recognize where the Lord stands and respect the position of God. There's a whole lot of mistakes that we make because we don't know what God says about the issue.

We do a lot of stuff because we've seen it done other places. And just because you see someone doing something and they look like they got it going on, doesn't mean they really do. You don't immediately see the effects of what they're doing in their life. God is slow to anger. So, if they're moving in error, He's not going to correct it right then on the spot. People continue to do wrong for years before you see it manifest.

People are always doing foolish stuff. And it looks as though they are succeeding and excelling. That's why the Bible tells us to "fret not" ourselves "because of evildoers, not be envious of workers of iniquity because they shall soon be cut down, like the grass and wither, like the green herb" (Psalm 37:1-2). In other words, He said, "Look, I know there are some people who aren't doing everything all together right, but it looks like they're prospering in spite of it." But what you have to do is recognize that God is going to take care of that. Your job is to make sure your life lines up with the Word of God. Sooner or later, they will start falling off because what they've done has caught up with them. And that's going to be the same time that God starts raising you up because you've been doing what is right in His sight. Encourage others and yourself daily to just keep doing right. Just keep standing where God says, and it's going to pay off. It may not be today. It may not be tomorrow, but you'll see after a while.

You normally do not see the effects of what you do immediately; it takes some time to manifest. So, even though something may be the way Daddy did it, and they try to tell you that as a man this is what you're supposed to do, if it's not God's position, you don't want to follow them if you want to be blessed. Psalm 1: says, "Blessed is the man that walketh not in the counsel of ungodly." In other words, if I want to be blessed, I've got to seek God's position and where He stands on the issue.

You have to respect this position. Fearing the Lord will cause you to respect His position.

Consider the following:

> "The fear of the Lord is the beginning of wisdom" (Psalm 111:10).

> "The fear of the Lord is the beginning of knowledge, but fools despise wisdom and instruction" (Proverbs 1:7).

> "The fear of the LORD is the beginning of wisdom: and the knowledge of the holy is understanding" (Proverbs 9:10).

> "If any of you lack wisdom, let him ask of God, that giveth to all men liberally, and upbraideth not; and it shall be given him" (James 1:5).

The reason why the fear of the Lord is the beginning of wisdom is because fearing God will begin to cause you to see the relevance of His plan. It will cause you to recognize that you can't even go to God and ask Him for certain things if you don't recognize and feel who He is.

We must strive for that reverence for God, understanding that for everything He does, there is a reason, plan, or purpose, and that we're not just here by accident. Once you begin to fear God and begin to develop that reverence and respect for Him, you begin to notice some other people walking around as though God doesn't exist.

I'm not talking about atheists. I'm talking about people who identify as Christians walking around and making all kinds of decisions and choices, never checking with God.

We must strive for that reverence for God, understanding that for everything He does, there is a reason, plan, or purpose, and that we're not just here by accident.

How many things do you do throughout the normal course of your and don't check with God to see how He feels about the matter? Of course, you don't have to check with Him to see if you should go to the bathroom or anything like that. But there's some stuff that you need to check with Him about when you make decisions.

The Bible says, "Trust in the LORD with all thine heart; and lean not unto thine own understanding. In all thy ways acknowledge him, and he shall direct thy paths" (Proverbs 3:5-6).

We can spend so much time trying to undo the mess we've made that we shouldn't have gotten into in the first place. Before you make a move or decision, ask yourself are you getting ready to do something stupid or not pleasing to God.

Acknowledge God first. Seek Him. Don't get out there on a limb and then try to bring Him in at the last minute. Check with Him in the beginning.

Proverbs 14:26 says, "In the fear of the LORD one has strong confidence, and his children will have a refuge."

So, start checking with God before making decisions or gaining new confidence to do stuff. For some people, it's lack of confidence that causes the stuff that you do to be in error. That's because you think you're being humble, but you're actually walking in doubt. And the Bible declares that anything done in doubt is sin.

Let's think about starting a business. If it be God's will for you to birth that business, but you birth it in doubt, it fails. It fails because the minute you start it, you have no confidence because you didn't check with God first. And since you don't have any confidence, you are uncertain if it will be successful. As soon as you believe that, it has failed and God can't bless it because it has become sin. You tainted and sabotaged your own endeavor from the very beginning.

Proverbs 14:27 states, "The fear of the LORD is a fountain of life, to depart from the snares of death." If you encounter something that is designed to take you out, fearing the Lord can be a fountain of life that's going to cause you to live in some situations.

When you fear God and you have trust and confidence in God, there's some endeavors that you can get into that were not supposed to work, but they do because the fear of the Lord is a *fountain*. That's the difference between people with and without fear of the Lord.

If God tells me to build a factory that makes cotton balls, I believe there is going to be an outbreak of earaches and my cotton balls factory is going to take off. Ask the Lord what does He want you to do. It doesn't matter what you do if your confidence is in the God I serve. Whatever you do is going to work.

I stand on the Word of God and go with it. I let it happen with God's help! Some of you are staying up all night questioning God about whether it's going to work. While you are worrying, we are working, and while you're guessing, we're making it happen. While you're changing direction, we are running ahead to see what the ending is going to be.

Refuse to hang with folks who are just as scared as you are. Have scary people in your presence? Tell them they have to go. Run with the big dogs instead. You don't have time to talk about "if," "when," or "maybe."

We've dealt a lot with fear. Fear of the Lord will cause you to develop a reliance on His provision. We want to rely on the provision of God. You won't work everything out yourself. But when you reverence God, the trust is there too. You know that God has your back.

Psalm 34:9 says, "O fear the Lord, ye his saints: for there is no want to them that fear him." Those that fear him lack for nothing. Verse 10 says, "The young lions do lack, and suffer hunger: but they that seek the Lord shall not want any good thing." Seek the Lord. Develop a relationship with Him where you can speak to Him directly. The preacher doesn't have to talk to God on your behalf. You have direct access.

Teaching you how to have a relationship with the Lord is what this book's about: to give you the Word. It is your job to execute it. I want you to take these words and use them to change your life right now. I want you to start doing things differently: start relying on God as your provision, see the relevance of His plan, and respect His position. I look forward to hearing the testimonies that will come from you checking with God before you make a decision on your own. Proverbs 19:23 declares, "The fear of the Lord tendeth to life: and he that hath it shall abide satisfied; he shall not be visited with evil." *Tendeth to life.* That means when I fear the Lord, He will take care of my life and he who has it shall abide satisfied. I learned that whatever is going on, I'm going to be all right. I've learned how to abide and be satisfied.

> *The preacher doesn't have to talk to God on your behalf. You have direct access.*

God is saying He's going to work it all out for you. He's going to give you what you need and make sure you are satisfied. The second half of that verse essentially says that there's some stuff the enemy won't even send your way because you fear God. Remind yourself that you can go through anything and be all God has destined you to be because He's already weeded out everything that will try to destroy you.Declare that no one can con you into believing that God is going to leave you high and dry because you are relying on His provision. Make a conscious effort to find out what He say about a situation before you make a decision. And then watch Him take care of you and keep you satisfied.

No matter what you're going through, stick to His plan knowing He won't leave you destitute. His plan will get you further ahead than you can on your own.

chapter 2

DEALING WITH DADDY'S DEVILS

Everybody has some devils. Now, theologically of course, there is only one devil, and there are several demons, which are fallen angels that plague mankind in an effort to get back at God. The devils we are talking about are not fallen angels, but they are forces that have plagued us for generations. But the core of the key scripture (Joshua 24) really speaks to a choice that Joshua is telling the children of Israel that they have to make at this point. They were in the right place at the right time; they are now walking in a promise, a benefit that was not made to them. But it *was* made to Abraham.

And that promise was handed down from Abraham, to Isaac, to Jacob. That promise survived the bondage of the Egyptians; that promise survived the Red Sea experience; that promise survived the wilderness wondering; that promise is now being manifested many generations later after bondage, after slavery, after wilderness, after a generation dies. Now these are the recipients of the promise that God has made to Israel. God's Word doesn't lie.

The Bible says He is faithful to perform what He has promised. And, so, through all the circumstances and situations that seemingly had Israel down and out, the promise survived.

Let's explain that just a little more. The promise survived the disobedience of Israel; the promise survived the trickery of Jacob; and the promise survived the 400+ years of bondage that the Egyptians were in. If that promise can survive all that, then God's promises can survive you making some bad choices.

His promises can survive you making some mistakes. His promises can survive you falling down. Now I'm trying to encourage you and let you know that even though sometimes we feel that we missed out on what God has for us because we haven't always been in the right place at the right time, it may take you longer to get there than a forty-day journey. It may take you forty years. But the promise will survive. Perhaps you haven't made all the right choices. God still has a plan for your life. His plan will survive our stupidity. His plan will outlast our stubbornness. His plan will outlast our bad decision-making. If there comes a time where we make up our mind to do right, and it's too late, our children will pick up where we left off. The promise will survive generations. That's why you decide that you're going to live right. That's why I'm going to serve the Lord. There's some stuff Daddy couldn't get because he was too stubborn. There was some stuff Granddaddy couldn't get either because he wouldn't change. But if we walk up right before God, not only will we get what God has promised us, but we will get the promise that survived that they couldn't receive. Your family has some unclaimed promises that you are in line to receive.

When we look back on our forefathers, they were the only example that we had. We all want to believe our mama did everything right. But there was some stuff Mama missed out on because she was stuck by habits and tradition. There was some good that Grandmama couldn't get done because the majority wouldn't vote on it. But we are free from the majority! We have been freed from tradition! We're in line not only to get what God has for each of us, but also stuff that God promised our families. If the negative attributes can carry over then the positive attributes can as well. One person may be crazy just like their momma. Another might be blessed just like their daddy.

Don't let anyone place negative spin on your family. You know your daddy wasn't a saint, but he was a good provider. Reject the bad and accept the good. It's a choice.

We all have some unclaimed stuff out there. It's what some people prayed for but didn't put themselves in line to get. However, God heard the prayer. So if God heard the prayer and moved on their behalf, but they didn't position themselves to claim it, the promises go to the heirs. It's like buying a house and never taking possession of it. Upon my demise, the house will go to my heirs.

Inheritance is not just an earthly or natural principle, but it's also a spiritual principle. This is why God made us His children because as joint heirs with Him, that entitles us to an inheritance. Some stuff that your forefathers prayed for that they didn't claim will become your inheritance if you walk up right before God. Don't become consumed with little trivial matters because there are promises and blessings floating around in the heavenlies with your name on them waiting for you to get in the right position. Joshua says what you're walking in right now is the product of what has come down through generations. You have been able to receive the blessings they did not. The reason they're in the Promised Land right now is because they were young. The older, unbelieving folk died out.

So, Joshua and Caleb are in the Promised Land. Sometimes when we're walking in the blessing, we don't recognize that it isn't always what we've done. But we are quick to assess where we are by what we're experiencing. And we operate under the old mantra, "If it isn't broke, don't try to fix it" because we haven't seen lightning flash and because we haven't lost everything. We think that everything is all good.

But Paul told the church at Corinth to notice that all of our fathers followed the cloud. All of them passed through the flood. But with many of them God wasn't well pleased, and they were overthrown in the wilderness. And, so, there is a distinction between deliverance and possessing the promise. All you must have is the desire to be delivered. But you must possess a certain lifestyle in order to receive the promise. That's why some people stopped short of achieving the promise.

If you don't do the bad things you used to anymore, you've been delivered. But all that was required for your deliverance was for you to call upon the name of the Lord. The Bible says, "For whosoever shall call upon the name of the Lord shall be saved" (Romans 10:13). All I had to do was talk to God about my issue. I got delivered, but then I have to change my lifestyle if I want to get the other stuff that He has for me.

So, we have to decide how are we going to act and live. Based on who our parents were and the environment that we grew up in, we may have a proclivity or a tendency to yield to certain things. The Bible says, "For I know that in me (that is, in my flesh,) dwelleth no good thing" (Romans 7:18). So you are fooling yourself if you believe otherwise. We know how to get dressed up for church and when to say Amen or Hallelujah, but there are still some things that we have to keep in check. The Bible reminds us to stay humble in 1 Corinthians 10:12; "Therefore let him that thinketh he standeth, take heed lest he fall."

Well, if you like jazz, can you go to the Jazz Festival? Sure. It's no sin, it's just music. But if music helped you through a struggle and music is tied to a special memory, you're not going because you like the music itself. You go because of the memories that the music generates. You know that music generates recall of memories because when you hear it play, all of a sudden you are back in that special place again.

Some songs you hear and instantly remember what you were doing, where you were, who you were with, and what was going down when that song had an impact. Our senses and spirit are tied to those memories.

Smells can do the same thing, especially certain familiar smells, like coffee. Whenever I smell coffee brewing, it always takes me back to my grandmother who passed away. We used to always spend the night at her house, and during the first week of school about four o'clock in the morning, you could smell coffee brewing. She would read the paper as soon as it hit the front driveway and we'd get up and that coffee smell would just waft into the room. We would have a little coffee, but it wouldn't always agree with us, and before the school bus came, we would wind up in the bathroom. It's amazing your how mind takes that trip back there.

That music or those smells awakened something. Something raised up and brought us back in time:

what we heard, what we used to do, what we did, and then after the song is over, you're back in the grown up you, but you have resurrected some old stuff. It leaves you smiling. There's some other baggage you may have too. You may have a dangerous proclivity to become an alcoholic if you have a family full of alcoholics. This is called familiar or familiar spirits. You're more susceptible to that disease, so you don't drink because that vulnerability is already in you.

The tendency to go there resides within you, which is why you can't start. Even if you never fell to this familiar spirt, you would want to let your children know because it's in them too. Well, I won't put my daughter on birth control because it's like I'm giving her a license to do as she pleases. I won't give my son protection for the same reason. You may be raising your children in church in the fear of the Lord, but you have to remember who you were in the past and how you got down. You also came up in church. As a matter of fact, it was with one of them in church.

So, 'put away the gods' doesn't say anything about coming to the altar to let somebody pray for you. Has it ever occurred to you that part of the reason why deliverance has not occurred may be because you keep asking God to do what *you're* supposed to do? *Lord, take this from me.* Well, put it away. It is a choice. We're talking about *service*. We're not talking about salvation.

He said serve the Lord. Now, I recognize that it's dangerous to talk about salvation in the context of Old Testament scripture because salvation as we know it has not become available yet. Jesus hasn't even been born. Calvary hasn't taken place. But the parallel is there. The parallel is that the people of Israel were God's chosen ones. And Galatians lets us know that we are the children of promise, just like Isaac. So, the relevance of the children of Israel to us in the church today is the fact that they were God's chosen people. We are now God's chosen people. But even in being chosen, you still have to choose sides.

In terms of accurately assessing these different times and dispensations, let's refer to the book of Romans to highlight some scriptural relevance. As discussed, we come up with all kind of excuses not to make changes. And so, when you're talking about changing some stuff in your life, you need to make sure you have the scriptural backup. Nobody's leaving you a loophole for a way out. You can't wiggle out of this one.

The devil can't make you do anything. Committing sin is our own choice.

Romans 6:14 says, "For sin shall not have dominion over you, for you are not under the law, but under grace." Sin doesn't have dominion over you. In other words, you can't act like the comedian Flip Wilson and say the devil made you do it. The devil can't make you do anything. Committing sin is our own choice. Joshua tells them to put away the gods of their father and choose to serve the true God. In the book of Hebrews, the 12th chapter, it tells us to lay aside every weight *and* sin.The Bible tells us we have authority over the enemy. Sin doesn't have dominion and because sin doesn't have dominion, if I resist the devil what's going to happen? He's going to flee because he can't make me do anything. I'm trying to give you your authority back. Because there are some things that we choose to deal with that God doesn't intend to have dominion in our lives.

For example, you never have to be the victim of abuse again. All the women in your family may have been in abusive relationships, but it can stop with you. Everyone in your family is struggling with poverty, but it can stop with you. Everyone in your family has high blood pressure. You don't have to have it. All the women had cancer or fibroid tumors. Again, it can stop with you. These ailments do not have dominion over you. My grandmother passed away from Alzheimer's, but that doesn't have to be my story.

When the enemy whispers thoughts that you will endure the same challenges, reject it in the name of Jesus. That is not God's will for your life. It is a choice; you do not have to accept it. No one controls what you experience in your life except you. Sin does not have dominion over you.If sin doesn't have dominion over me, then I need to find out where the dominion lies. If we go back to Genesis 1:26, God says, "Let man have dominion."

God has given us dominion. That's what's awesome about salvation because salvation has nothing to do with my pedigree. We try to use or discard people based on where they come from or what family they're from. Let me tell you something: I could come from a family full of folks who are not good, yet be a strong Christian myself. People say about me all the time, "Well, you know, he's a third-generation preacher."

I don't care if somebody is a first-generation preacher and the past two generations were not. God has given that person dominion.

On the other hand, you can come from a family of preachers and be out on the street selling drugs. So, your pedigree means nothing. God has given us each the authority to take our life back, take life by the reins, and strive to be all God has purposed for us to be.

I'm not even going to let others put me in a box with a label. God has some plans and I'm not going to let anyone limit me. To sum this up: the sky is your limit. Put away or lay aside some stuff this week.

The first thing I said this morning was "I'm going to drop this (physical) weight. I'm putting it away." A couple of brothers and I were talking recently. We were saying that I can do it whenever I want to; all I have to do is put it away. But many times, a lot of the stuff that we do that passes for trying, is actually not trying *for real.*

You want to go back to school? You can do it if you really want to. You want a better life? You can do it if you want to. You want to live holy? You can do it if you want to. We always conjure up excuses to try to justify everything, but no one is holding you back. 'Well, you know, I *would* do it if....' Well, that's all right. Your child will pick it up; somebody down the line will pick it up.

A God-anointed prophet came to me once and we were talking and he told me some stories. And it didn't make sense to me until the Lord started dealing with me about this. He said, "There's something in your family that's come down—lies and somewhere along the way you walked into an anointing that wasn't really intended for you to have."

I responded, "What?" He said, "Yes, you walked into an anointing that wasn't intended for you. Somebody in your family told me about it." Then he described this situation I was dealing with. He said that when I went through this, I made a decision that caused me to inherit some stuff spiritually.

The story of Elijah and Elisha told in 2 Kings 2:11-14, shows us how mantles or anointing can be transferred. The interesting part of the story is not the transfer itself but how it was transferred. When Elijah was taken up, the Bible says that the mantle fell to the ground. Then Elisha picked the mantle up and began to operate in it. We are able to pick up the mantles, blessings, and anointing of those who have come before us. To be clear, I am not talking about being blessed by ancestors, like some may believe. However, the Bible says in Hebrews 11 that there were some believers that prayed for things and died in faith not having received them. So, when they don't receive it where does it go? Abraham did not live to see some of the things that were promised but Joshua and the children are standing in the promise.

There have been prayers offered up that you are able to benefit from. We all stand on the shoulders of those who have come before us. You may not be the first one in your family to serve the Lord. But you're going to be the first one to walk into certain things. So, get ready.

How do I know if I'm getting ready walk into an inheritance? I'm not going to shout my way into it. I'm going to *live* my way right into it. We are able to do that and experience God moving exceeding abundantly above anything we could imagine.

If that happens, it's could cause some confusion because you will start tracing your steps and trying to figure out what you did to really deserve what God wants to do. And when you look at your life and recognize that nothing can really account for what God is trying to do, you just say, "Oh, God, I thank you that somehow I was in the right place. Somehow, I listened to something. I thank you that out of all the stuff I disobeyed, the one thing I got right has caught on."

We've all made some bad decisions. And there's been some times when you weren't where you were supposed to be. But you say, "God, for whatever reason, I am glad you're doing what you're doing right now." I thank God that I had sense enough in that moment to say yes. I thank God that I had sense enough in that season to be obedient. And as a matter of fact, I'm cautious now about everything I do. I don't want to mess it up.

Even if you're not a first-generation churchgoer, you may be part of the first generation trying to live right. And many of us have been hurt and wounded in church. Some folks have been hurt by family members who held positions of power. It's totally fair to ask, "How are they supposed to be this and they're doing me like that? How are they supposed to be that and treating me like this?"

What you don't recognize is even though they have messed up, they were laying up some treasures in the heavenlies. And because they didn't receive them, you're getting ready to walk right into a spiritual inheritance.

You can proclaim, "I will walk into the favor. I'm getting ready to walk into some favor of the forefathers of some folk that came before me. I am not going to do the foolishness that they did. If some blessings are coming down, then I'll be getting ready to walk right into them."

But there's a choice to be made. And there are some things that you have to make the decision to put away. Stop looking for someone to come take it from you. Put it away, because when you put it away, it shows God that you're willing to make the commitment—the lifestyle commitment—to receive what He has for you.

Don't let this opportunity pass you by. You have to choose what you're going to put away. Not only that, you have to choose what you're going to pick up. You might need to start studying your family lineage. There may be some blessings, sometimes that you're even praying for already. And you need to tap into that anointing because God does move within families.

Remember, your family doesn't have to operate in the anointing for Him to anoint *you*. But there are some blessings that may be specific. And there's a specific anointing that may be tied to your family.

Recognize not only the negative things that are familiar or that you may have a tendency to fall into, but an anointing that your family tends to flow in. Discover what that anointing is. Paul told Timothy that he wasn't even aware of the anointing that was in him. He said, "I know it's in you, Timothy, because it was in your mother Lois and your grandmother Eunice." Because it was in them, he said, I know it's in you, too.

Take time to explore some of the trends of your family. I'm going back and studying that for myself and I'm going to dig it up. Let me see who this one was and who that one was and figure out how God flows through them.

chapter 3

HOW TO STAND FOR THE HOUSE

Going back to our foundational scripture of Joshua 24:15, we're going to just examine the latter portion of that verse that we should just about know by heart. It says, "...but as for me and my house, we will serve the Lord."

We want to begin dealing with taking a stand for the house. We recognize first and foremost that the statement that Joshua makes at this juncture in our scriptural text, is the beginning of a stand.

"We are going to serve the Lord" doesn't mean that you *are* serving Him. You have acknowledged your intent but now you have to follow through.

You need to understand that it's not just all talk, even though what you say does matter. Life and death is in the power of the tongue. But you must recognize that standing is not simply declaring your intent but is the *follow through*.

Don't just talk about it. A lot of times we have good ideas and we're quick to say what we're going to do. You need to be slow to speak... don't talk so much. We get into worship and we feel the presence of the Lord moving. And we start saying all the stuff we're going to do differently. But you need to understand when you leave the manifested presence of God and you go home and reality sets in, and you have to deal with the day-to-day struggles, you are bound by what you have spoken.

> *...while we seek to impress people with our conversation, God is impressed by our follow through actions.*

That's why you can't let other folks hype you up, and get you saying what *you're* believing God for and you truly don't believe Him for that.

When we move in our Christian circles around other people that profess to believe, we try to 'out talk' one another. But what we fail to realize is that we have to be able to live up to the level of our profession. You have to follow through with your lifestyle up to the level of the things that you've spoken. If you say, "I believe God," life is going to test whether or not you truly believe in Him. "God, I trust you. I'm going to stand on your word." Well guess what? You're going to have to do that. And what we fail to realize is that while we seek to impress people with our conversation, God is impressed by our follow through *actions*.

A lot of times, it's not because we didn't have faith enough when we spoke it. But somewhere along the way, we walked away from our faith. You need to understand it's not going to happen instantaneously. *God, I want it done. I want you to do it right now.* Some things The Lord will do right now; some things, however, require a *process*. And the process is necessary whenever there are multiple factors that the Lord is trying to work out all at the same time.

It's not just about you getting what you need. If it was just you getting what you need, you would simply ask for it and you receive it immediately. But in order to get what you need, you also have to develop a level of character so that you can maintain what God gives you. When you get it, you want to keep it.It's frustrating to move to a blessed place and then have to leave for whatever reason. You'll be better off not ever having gone there than to have to go there and leave. Lots of folks struggle financially. You don't see us killing ourselves. We are not having nervous breakdowns, we not tripping out about money because for many of us, money has always been tight. But you take a person that has been able to do whatever they want to do, whenever they get ready, with all the money or disposable income that they want and then put them in some other shoes, they would trip out and not be able to handle it. So that's why it's important that we be able to endure the process and have an understanding about what God is trying to accomplish in our lives, so that when we get to whatever the next place is, it can be maintained.

Let me tell you first what the next place is *not*.

God, I'm going to the next level. You think the next level is a place where you don't have any bills? That place doesn't exist.

Well, you can be debt free, but debt free includes the understanding that there are certain debts that are not going to go away because they keep getting renewed. Yes, some bills you will always have. You will always have to pay taxes. You always have to deal with some form of insurance. So, whether it's life insurance, health insurance, or car insurance, you will always have premiums. If you live in the state of Virginia, you will always have personal property taxes.

We need to understand that debt free is not the same as free of obligations. You're not going to get to the point where you don't have to pay anybody. That's only the case if you end up in jail somewhere. So, if you looking for that place, you're going to have to relocate and probably do something illegal.

Now, I don't want to burst your bubble. You *can* get to the place where your house and car are paid off. Less debt is good, but there's some stuff, you will always have. That's just obeying the laws of the land and supporting yourself and your family. That's just the way that it goes.

God's going to give you the strength to endure some things that you just have to deal with. You may have transitioned to the next place or the another level and may not even recognize it.

As you try to get to the next level, life around you seems to be going crazy. You wonder why you feel under attack. You're dealing with attacks that you've never dealt with before. *Welcome to the next place.*

> *The next place is another place spiritually. As you grow and mature spiritually, you're going to prosper in the natural world as well.*

Well I thought it was going to get better. It will once you master this place. The reason it was easy before is because you mastered where you were. The next place is not a physical or geographic location. The next place is another place *spiritually*. As you grow and mature spiritually, you're going to prosper in the natural world as well. But when God prospers you in the natural world, it's a direct reflection of your spiritual growth. Now, when you move to another level or another place spiritually, you need to understand the scenery may look the same, but there will be some stuff revealed to you that was hidden previously.

Some demonic forces are going to be revealed that you didn't see previously because the enemy is around you. But you're not privy to a lot of it because you're not strong enough to handle it. So, you're prevented from having to deal with certain attacks because you haven't matured yet to the place where you can handle it. Anything that's revealed to you, you have to know that you're spiritually strong enough to overcome it.

That's a lot to chew on. *I don't know why I hadn't seen this. I don't know why all this stuff seems like it is going crazy.* You couldn't handle it before, but now that you're on another level, you're able to deal with some things. You're dealing with things from another perspective; you're dealing with things in another realm. Another level of spirituality and spiritual warfare has now opened up and you are now exposed to some things that you didn't see before. Before you got along with everybody in the ministry. Everybody was just so sweet, so kind, so loving. Now you're starting to see that every person who was showing his or her teeth wasn't smiling.

Some of those looks were snarls. And it's not looking as nice and as loving as it did before. Some new things are being revealed, but that's because you matured to the point where you can handle it. As you mature, the first thing that's going to happen are problems that we're not problems previously are going to reveal themselves.

If the Lord showed you some of the stuff that you would have to deal with and some of the stuff that was around the corner for you before you matured spiritually, you would run for the hills.

But if it's been revealed and exposed, then you are strong enough to overcome it. And you may not always feel that way. That's why sometimes the enemy gets the best of you. You may give in and not pull out what's in you. But if it's revealed, you can handle it. So you need to know that that first of all, what you speak is not the beginning and end of you standing but it is a process. Now we're going to deal with the process of standing for the house. And the first thing you need to know when standing is that it's important that you maintain your profession.

chapter 4

MAINTAIN YOUR PROFESSION

The maintenance of your profession is essential. We've taken the stand and proclaimed, ". . . as for me and my house, we're going to serve the Lord." Now that we've spoken it out of our mouths, it's important that we maintain what we have spoken.

Be careful and don't back up. The Bible declares that life and death is in the power of the tongue. Once you speak it, the devil is going to come and try to make you back up off of what you've spoken. When I speak it, a tug of war over me begins. The enemy is on deadline. The only time he has to deal with my profession is in the time between when I speak it and when it comes to pass.

Remember that when we declare that our house is the house of God, and our family will serve the Lord, that's a declaration of war. That's the first blow in the battle. Now the enemy is operating on a timeline. He has to launch a demonic onslaught. He's got to send his imps at you to break you because life and death is in the power of your tongue. When you made the declaration, you spoke life. It's the devil responsibility to throw everything he can at you to make you speak death. I've been given the authority to speak. Hebrews 10:23 tells us to hold fast to our profession of faith without wavering.

That means I cannot waver concerning what I've said that God will do. It says don't waver. Why? What does the last part of verse 23 say? "For He is faithful, that promised." So now why would the Hebrew writer have to convince me that God is faithful? That's your insight right there into the devil's plan and his attack. If you have to tell somebody that God is faithful, what must they be going through at that point in time?

For the Hebrew writer to say God is faithful and that He's going to do what He promised, that must mean the attack is designed to convince me that God is not going to do what He said He would do. If the enemy cannot stop God from doing it, and he can't change what I've spoken, what is the purpose of him attacking?

I must hold fast the profession of my faith, without wavering. The enemy does not have to get me to say God's not going to do it. All he has to do is get me to waver. That is his objective. He cannot take the authority from you. He can't stop God from doing it. But if he can get you to waver, then it will cancel out what you have spoken. The devil's not a creator or a builder, but a wrecking ball.

He's a pervert and he twists out of shape the things that God has designed to work for our good. I'm going to show you the perversion. James 1:6-7 says, "But let him ask in faith, nothing wavering. For he that wavereth is like a wave of the sea driven with the wind and tossed. For let not that man think that he shall receive anything of the Lord." So, if the enemy can cause me to waver, then I can't get anything accomplished.

> *The devil's not a creator or a builder, but a wrecking ball.*

You must hold fast and maintain your profession. James 1:8 declares, "A double minded man is unstable in all his ways." Wavering represents instability. If I'm unstable, I'm not standing, am I?

We have to understand and recognize that once we speak what we believe about God, the enemy is going to come immediately to try and cause us to waver. Understand that the enemy is coming and your situation may actually begin to look worse. You think that maybe you should have never spoken what you believe. Maybe God isn't going to do it or maybe you heard the Lord wrong. May I suggest that you didn't hear Him wrong, but it's the enemy beating you up until you begin to waver. And once you begin to waver, he can cancel the good news. When you waver, you become unstable and cancel out the good that God is trying to do for you. Consider Romans 14:23 which is where the perversion comes in. I've spoken it. But if I don't continue to believe and maintain my profession, scripture says, "And he that doubteth is damned if he eat, because he eateth not of faith: for whatsoever is not of faith is sin." The magnitude of that is huge. Whatever is not of faith is sin!So, how many things do we do without believing God for it?

How many things do we do that are just analytical by nature? It's a good idea, but if I've not checked with God, I am not believing God. The Bible says in Hebrews 11:1, "Faith is the substance of things hoped for." The Bible says in Romans 8:24, "For what a man seeth why doth he yet hope for?" So if faith is the substance of things hoped for, faith is designed to get me to the thing that I can't see, that I can't devise a plan for, that I can't connect the dots of and get to on my own.

That's why some of us are stuck in so many trials and tribulations and go through the same thing over and over again. By not doing it in faith, doing only what's comfortable, we're not getting to the next place.

We can pray and ask God for something that He already promised. And the minute you begin to waver, it becomes sin. The minute you begin to doubt God and start counting how many things you prayed for, you've backed up off it. *Maybe that isn't what the Lord wants me to have. Maybe that's not what I committed to.* You let the enemy pervert it, and you end up with nothing.

For many of us, the moment we step out of faith is when our faith is at its peak, but we don't keep feeding our faith. We begin to feed all that negativity. But in order to maintain your profession, you've have to stop listening to people who use words like "can't" that are negative and always talk about the worst outcomes.

Well, what if it doesn't work? What if it *does* work? Why do you have to look at it from that negative perspective? You cannot feed yourself those thoughts and words and expect a change. There are some folks even in church that you need to stop talking to because they don't ever have anything positive to say. God's blessing and healing is moving all around them and all they can identify is the one thing that's wrong. You need to stop talking to them because they aren't going anywhere. They're miserable, they're bitter, and they're trying to take you with them.

Resolve that you will not let anything or anyone pull you down after you've spoken your faith. Get around some folks who are going to believe God and are going to edify you and encourage you to let you know that with God all things are possible. Some people have no reason to believe because they haven't spoken anything good. Tell them you have no time to listen to their negative self.

There's no one I talk to more during the course of the day than my wife. That's because nobody's got on the line what we got on the line.

We all need someone that's going to tell us it's going to be all right. And then I'm going to *tell her* it's going to be all right. Then she will tell me God is able; then I will tell her God is able. We may have to encourage each other several times each day. She may call me when I'm up, and she's down. She may call back later when I'm down and she's up. We do what we have to do to get through the day because we cannot go back on what we've spoken; there's too much riding on it.

Until you come into the knowledge that God has something better for you than where you are, you can't see yourself beyond this place. Other people can see it all over you while you're moping around looking all pitiful, like you're the only one going through what everybody's going through.

Refuse to stop believing and keep going.

Announce to your loved ones: "I can't stop here." The worse it gets, the more motivated you ought to be to keep going now. You may slow down a little bit when it gets good. But you're not going to stop there. You have to learn how to maintain what you say. And keep believing. You have to keep hoping until the end. And every day your hope is going to be stronger. Stop being pessimistic and spotting the negative in everything. Don't think *Well, God didn't do it yesterday, what makes me think He's going to do it today?* You have to flip that thing and say He didn't do it yesterday, but today, I'm one step closer to God working it out. I'm one step further in the process. I'm one step closer to getting what God has promised me. My glass is half full, not half empty. Learn and listen. If the devil is strategic in trying to break you apart, you have to be strategic in lifting yourself up.

Get all hate out of your spirit. Surround yourself with some people that have already been through what you're going through. Stop dealing with the pitiful people in the same place; they can't encourage you while they need encouragement themselves. It's best to get around those that have come through it. They will be your living example of if God did it for them, surely He can do it for me. Lay down your pride. Put jealousy aside. You're going to have to be open about what you're going through. Some folks want everybody to help them, but they can't appreciate anybody else. The Lord won't open a door for people until their heart changes. He puts people around us not to make us mad, but to encourage and motivate each other.

> *If the devil is strategic in trying to break you apart, you have to be strategic in lifting yourself up.*

You may feel like everywhere you look, it seems like everyone's being blessed, but you are left out. Maybe the Lord has surrounded you with those people to let you know that if you get your heart right, you're next! You may be sick and don't want to be around others because it seems like everyone is doing well except you. Get the jealousy and hate out of your mind. Don't be enslaved to your mind and your thoughts. As an African American I can say that one of the major things that slavery did to our community was to turn us against one another.

That physical weeping and torment was in the past, but the most grueling, lasting effects are in the mess we still deal with now. We are in danger of becoming what they called us. We keep trying to pull each other down. And that's not God's intent for us.

The message of the Kingdom is the message of grace, that if God can do it for someone that looks like you, that had the same hang ups as you do, the same issues as you have, it ought to give you hope. But some of us have traded in our hope for hate. Then we're upset when we are the cause for being where we are.

God is always getting ready to do something. And some folks cheat their way right out of a blessing. Some talk themselves right into it. But some people are going to talk their way right out of it.

You should be joyful because God has everything in place. Confess it out loud: "He's got it all in place." All you have to do is keep on. When you speak it out of your mouth, it begins a series of events to bring it to pass.

All you need to do now is keep walking. And you are going to walk right into provision and blessing. Walk right through that open door. If you maintain your profession, you're going to keep walking and walk right into what God has for you. You won't have to look for it or chase it down. All you have to do is keep walking.

God said that it's not too much for Him. He's going to do what He said and more.

And once He performs, your faith is at its ultimate level. You have moved to another place of faith. So you begin to believe that He can move the next mountain. You go looking for mountains to move just because you can. You go to the meanest person on your job and tell them they are going to be your personal project, and before much time pasts, they are coming to church with you and walk down the aisle to give their life to Christ. This is how the Lord's trying to get you to the place where you go looking for challenges. And your faith is mature to the point where after you declare your intent, you start walking in the direction of that better move and you actually get there.

Right now, you may still be kind of shaky. *Lord, you have me out there. I have to stand because if I waver, I'll gain nothing.* Hang in there and know that the Lord is doing it to try to teach you something and once you come through this, your faith is going to move to another place once God shows you. This could be the turning point in your life.

Once you understand the process, you'll start believing even more. The major breakthrough comes when you start believing for other people. Rightyou're your faith may not be strong enough to believe on others' behalf. But when God moves for you, things change. You're in a different place spiritually and will begin to pray and believe for others. Please understand that the Lord is trying to build something great in you. He's developing some stuff in you, and so first you have to learn how to maintain; you have to learn how to maintain your profession.

chapter 5

MANIPULATE YOUR PERSPECTIVE

The second important thing that you must learn to do when standing for the house is learning to manipulate your perspective. You have to learn how to change your position so that you can see things differently. Things look a certain way depending upon where you're standing, and when you change your perspective, things don't always look the same. Resolve to maintain your profession and stop trying to back up off of what you promised.

The Bible asks us to serve the Lord. "Choose you this day whom ye will serve, whether the gods which your father served were on the other side of the river, or the gods of the Amorites in whose land ye dwelled. But as for me and my house, we will serve the Lord."

In a previous example, I explored the process of standing for the house. *The process.* I've come to realize why we don't like processes. We live in an instantaneous, microwave society and want things done instantly. We may say things like, "I want to do it one time be done with it." I want to show up at church with my family and my spouse who's been messed up all their life should be perfect now."

That's silly, right? But that's how we think. Everything at home might be good for about a week or so with the kids just acting right.

Then notes are sent home from school because the kids aren't listening. A bill pops up out of nowhere.

Money that we had earmarked for something dwindles. Money that was put aside to do a little shopping for the holiday is gone because a bill that I thought I paid arrives. Then the add on a late fee. Unexpected life situations threaten to set us off.

We have to be real because a lot of times while hearing sermons or reading good material, we understand the *theory*. We get how it's *supposed* to work. But we don't get the process of working that thing out, working through the bumps and the bruises until I see how it's supposed to be, and *understand* how it's supposed to work. But it's a process of getting from where I am to where

I need to be. There is a process that I have to undergo to get things from where they are to where they are supposed to be.

It's easier when you're just dealing with *you*, because you can change and grow at whatever rate you choose based on the level of your commitment and sincerity. Some people come to Christ and instantly drop all their bad habits. They stop smoking, stop drinking, and stop cussing, and stop all that other stuff. But for some people, it takes a while. That doesn't mean that they are any less sincere about their commitment.

Just because God might have delivered you from crack instantly, doesn't mean it can *only* happen that way. For this other person, it took a 12-step program. Does that mean because it took you one step and took them 12 steps, that they're really not saved? No. Understand that based on who you are and your circumstances, the process is different for each individual. So, when we start talking about 'standing for the house,' and making our families and our homes what God has purposed for them to be, you have some other variables in the equation.

Again, it's easier when it's you by yourself, when you just got to get *you* right. It's a different story when there's some other folks in the equation. You have children and a spouse and they are not growing at the rate that you're growing. They don't respond the way that you respond. And it's different for men and women. If you have a man who's committed, he might understand why this is how it is, and that this is how it's supposed to be, then just let it be at that. Everything has got emotional tie-ins, though, and women pay more attention to them.

Is that a responsibility thing when I stop doing this bad thing? I know that if the Lord said I don't need to do this, and if I don't do this, then he's going to bless my family and me. So, it's more of a logical move for the man in terms of responsibility, to think, *This this is why I want to take this step. Let's make it happen so it can get done.* But for women it's a little different.

That doesn't mean it's worse. For some brothers, when something happened as fast as we think it ought to happen, we may pull back. But for a lot of women, there are a lot of emotions tied into your actions. You may act a certain way because there is an emotional connection. So, while you know that you need to let this go or move away from something in order to get to the next place, there's a pain in me that has to be healed, so that I can release what I'm holding onto that's hindering me from getting to the next level. For women, it's a logical, sensible move. Normally, there has to be an emotional disconnect with whatever it is that's causing you trouble.

There's a reason why we do the things we do. And there's a reason why we grow at the rate that we grow. A brother can come to church and all you have to do is give him the Word and a good worship service. He doesn't have to know anybody around him; nobody needs to talk to him.

But the woman has to feel like she's embraced. She has a need to feel like she fits in. She thinks *When they look at me, but don't really talk to me, I don't feel like I belong.* For the brother, he doesn't have to belong. All he needs is the Word to point him in the direction of what he needs to do to get to the next place. We're built differently. The same messages are not received the same way by all. This is where the challenge comes in for families because we have to get the whole house to this place. We talked about how we have to be in agreement and how the enemy's going to try to bring division in our homes.

One of the ways that division intrudes is because we don't understand how the other person operates or emotes. We expect the other person to function like us. People who struggle with the same stuff that you've been delivered from, you don't understand why they haven't been delivered yet. *Well, if I got over it, why can't they get over it?* The answer is: they are not you.

They're built differently, and that doesn't mean that they don't love God. But it means that there are some other issues behind the scenes that have not been resolved. They haven't gotten to that place. You have to reach out to people. That's what's amazing about God. He *understands it all.*

Sometimes you just need someone to understand you. You might explain, "I don't need anybody to feel sorry for me; I don't need your pity. I just need you to understand me, because if you can just understand how I tick then you will know that that I'm not as bad as I appear to be."

It can be helpful to tell a trusted family member: "I'm not as messed up as you think. It's just some things the Lord is still trying to work out in me." So, when we're standing for the house, we recognize that it's not just a one-time thing, but it's a process. I have to continue to stand every day; I have to stand in every decision. With every decision that you make, you're taking a stand.

Either you're going to do it God's way or not. That's the decision that you're making. In every decision you make, every move you make, it's not just one moment. "When it's time to decide whether I'm going to hold my peace or go off, I'm taking a stand. In the heat of the battle, I have to decided whether I'm going to be tactful and try to be a peace maker, or if I'm going to say the one thing I know will hurt you.

I have learned why we shouldn't argue.

The point of an argument is not to bring about a happy resolution. The point of any argument is to win. You say whatever it takes to win. But nobody really wins because somebody is going to end up hurt. And the person that appears to win is usually the one that cares the least about peaceful resolution.

"There are clever things I could say that would put you down. Yet I will restrain myself because I love you too much to really hurt you like that."

When you're in a relationship with somebody, you know what buttons to push to send them over the top. There are some folks that you can say certain things to, and you know if you say it, they will never recover, whether it's true or not.

In everything we do, including the secret, quiet conversations we have that nobody else knows about, in *those* things, we're taking a stand. Sometimes in church, we may act like and look like we're serving God, but behind the scenes, we may not be standing. Then we want God to stand for us. But we haven't been standing for him.

One of the neatest things I heard another preacher say is: "When I tell you something, if I say it once, I'll say it again." He said it all the time. And it meant that I'm not going to tell you something in secret that I won't tell you out loud. But a lot of us don't really want to be caught doing the things we talk about.

Yet we wonder why we're losing our testimony. We wonder why the people that live in the very same house with us don't support what we've been called to do. They don't want to believe. Our children don't want to believe what we believe because they don't see it working for us.

The hardest people to win over are the people that live in the house with you. That's because they see both sides. So, we have to *learn* to take a stand even when nobody's looking. It's a process.

We might have a good time when we come to church. We cry, we lift our hands, and we make a profession to God. "I want you to change this. I want you to move. I want you to do this." But then when we leave, we don't continue to honor what we said at the altar.

We talked about maintaining our profession—the words we speak out of our mouth that we believe God and what He wants to do. You have to learn how to maintain that profession. You have to work, you have to live, you have to speak, and you have to operate each day and make decisions and choices based on what you profess that you wanted God to do.

Mark 11:24 says, "Whatsoever things we desire when we pray, believe that we receive them and we shall have them." In other words, when I pray, in order for me to have it, I must have the belief that I will receive it. If you believe that God is going to turn your life around, then your conversation ought to support the fact that it's already turned around. It doesn't matter what it looks like. It matters what I *believe*. When things started looking better, then you got it. No. Believe that you've already received it. You have to see the change before it manifests.

See the change in your finances. See the change in your children; see the change in your spouse; see the change in your home. See the change in whatever it is that you desire.

It may seem crazy to you, but we're not walking by what we see. We're walking directed by *faith*: acting as though it's done and the change has already taken place.

God, I want a loving relationship. I want my spouse to stop all this fussing and I want us to live in harmony. So why do you always wait for the change to come in the other person?

If I act like it's already done, then that means you can't argue with me. It doesn't mean that you can't ever trip out, but you can't argue with me because I refuse to argue back. If I refuse to argue back, then there is no argument.

Looking for the other person to change and thinking that when they act right, I'll start acting like I'm supposed to act is the wrong approach.

Not only do you have to maintain your profession, you have to learn to manipulate your perspective. Change the way you see the world.

When you manipulate your own perspective, it doesn't change what happened, but it changes the way you view it. Sometimes that's all you need is to change your point of view—manipulate the perspective by changing the way that you see a situation. You might be looking at it wrong or missing something.

Now let's go to Romans because it will make you look differently at scriptures you quote all the time. This is one of the most famous passages that people quote. Romans 8:28 says, "And we know that all things work together for good to them that love God, to them who are the called according to his purpose." If all things work together for my good, why am I getting bent out of shape when stuff goes wrong? You have to realize that even the wrong things are part of what works together for you. We know that *all* things are not just the blessings, benefits, perks, and increase, but also the hard times, the problems, the obstacles, the being talked about, feeling like I'm alone in the struggle, going through storms, valleys, and all the pain that we try to avoid. It's *all* working together for my good. It may not be or feel good, but it's still working for my good. This should inspire us to change the way you view storms and problems, trials and tribulations. If I'm walking according to the will of God, then even though it may be uncomfortable for me during this season, it's still working for my good.

But usually, we let our problems bend us all out of shape like we don't know or believe the Word of God that we quote. *I can't believe this is going on, Lord. I don't know, where are you God?* Rest assured it's working for your good!

The Lord delights in blessing you. Instead of complaining, keep walking and moving. Stay with the process so that at the end you will receive what you've been praying for. If not, you're still in the same place, and nothing has been gained from your storms and trials. They were supposed to work for your good but you couldn't endure the process. And it's because your perspective is wrong. Romans 8:5 says, "For they that are after the flesh do mind the things of the flesh; but they that are after the Spirit the things of the Spirit." You cannot see what God is doing if you continue to mind the things of the flesh. Yet the Lord said, "All things are working together for the good to them that love God, to them who are the called according to his purpose." That means even in my storms, even in my hardships, God's hand is in it.

He didn't send the problem; He didn't send the issue, but He has tempered the storm. He has tempered my difficulty so that I can take it. All the stuff that you can't take has already been weeded out. Things like you are going to give up or have a nervous breakdown have all been weeded you. You won't break through to the good unless you keep speaking it. You break down because you want to be broken down.

The fact of the matter is all the stuff that you couldn't take—troubles that would have put you over the edge into the deep end—that would cause you to lose your mind, has been filtered out. It has been weeded out and God has tempered your storm not so that it will break you, but it will mold you to stop resisting the hand of God trying to set you to be what He's called you to be.

We're talking about manipulating your perspective. Some of you make it easy for others to know what your perspective is. You wear it all over your face. Joy is lacking, you don't have a praise, and you're just broken down. But you tell others that you are fine and alright. And, truthfully, who isn't just as messed up as you. You don't want to let anyone know you're going through, but your facial expressions and demeanor tell a different story.

Keep in mind that your perspective determines your attitude. The way to move God is with thanksgiving. If you want God to move, you should start telling Him, "Thank you."

In the midst of what you're going through, if view it from the spirit, you know it's working together for your good, so be thankful even for the storm because you already know the outcome.

Philippians 4:8 states, "Finally, brethren, whatsoever things are true, whatsoever things are honest, whatsoever things are just, whatsoever things are pure, whatsoever things are lovely, whatsoever things are of good report; if there be any virtue, and if there be any praise, think on these things."

> *The way to move God is with thanksgiving. If you want God to move, you should start telling Him, "Thank you."*

It doesn't say whatever things are a fact. It says whatever things are *true*. There is a difference between truth and facts. Facts change, the truth doesn't. The fact may be that you are going through something right now. But the truth is that you are an overcomer. The fact may be that your money is tight right now. But the truth is that God will supply. The fact may be that the doctor gave you a bad news report. But the truth is that you're already healed.

So, we have to focus not on the facts, because the facts change with every situation. But the truth remains consistent throughout any situation. The fact is I may be in a storm right now. But the truth is it's going to work together for my good. It may be uncomfortable, but the truth is that it's going to work for my good. We just have to manipulate our perspective.

If it's looking bad and you continue looking at the facts of the situation, you may start to get depressed, sad, and down in the dumps. It is then that you have to make the decision to change the way you are looking at the situation. The scripture says to focus on those things that are true; those things that are real. Whatever things are real mean you cannot look at what the enemy is presenting because all he is presenting is an illusion and a perversion of the truth.

You have to understand that the enemy is a liar. He perverts truth. He twists it. So, he's going to present to you a perverted version of the truth. The truth is that things are changing. But he's going twist that change to make it look like it's getting worse instead of getting better. Please understand this transition is not comfortable. So, while you're moving and changing and things become unfamiliar, the enemy will try to convince you that it's getting worse, you aren't doing things right, and you should bail. But the devil is a liar!

The truth is that your situation is getting better because it's what God promised you. So, hold on to the truth. Believe the report of the Lord. Hold on to what's real and honest regardless of how it looks in the natural. Your mind is not in the things of the flesh but in the things of the Spirit. Do what is right even when it looks like doing what's wrong with get you ahead.

A hookup or trying to skip some steps of the process will get you caught in a bad place. You must always do what's right even though it may seem you're moving backwards. The saying is that "desperate times call for desperate measures," but Christians are never desperate. Some stuff just doesn't apply to who we are. As believers, we are never desperate. So desperate measures are never a necessity.

When the enemy comes in, it's the standard of God that's going to protect you. You may have walked away from God's standard and that leaves you vulnerable to the attack of the enemy. But you now know the tricks of the enemy. Keep forging ahead and get all God has promised you "Whatever things are pure and whatever things are lovely." You have to learn to see the good and to see God in all things. Some folks have talked trash and they've rubbed you the wrong way. But you have to look and see the good in them, too, because the Lord saw the potential in *you*. When you were lost, He saw the potential in you when other folks didn't want to deal with you.

When you see the good in them, it will cause you to pray for them instead of casting them to the side. It will cause you to give them another chance and have compassion instead of just not dealing with them anymore. You must get to the place and point where you start seeing the pure stuff, where you start seeing things that are lovely, the things of good report.

Stop letting folks come to you with everything that's negative, with everything that's wrong. You're not a dumping ground for people's complaints or dirty laundry. If someone doesn't have anything uplifting to say, don't give them time to fill your heard with thoughts that are going to send you down the wrong path. Then the Bible says that if there be any virtue, it's the spirit of excellence, and if you're going to be excellent, there will be praise.

The way that you're going to have joy and the way you will be able to operate in excellence and not in desperation is by changing your perspective. You've got to manipulate your perspective when you find yourself getting down or when you find yourself ready to give up. Change the way that you see things and look at the situation from a different outcome.

Ask for God's help seeing a divine hand in it. *Help me to see how you're working it together for my own good. I know that your hand is on me. And if your hand is on me, then it's got to be on my situation. Help me to see how you're working and molding me; help me to see how you are changing me. Manipulate my perspective until I can rejoice while going through tough times; until I can smile even when I feel like I'm crying. Manipulate my perspective so that I can give praise even in the midst of my storm.*

Whatever the situation is usually isn't as bad as you think it is. As a matter of fact, you're closer to coming out than you realize. Just change your perspective. Look at it differently because the enemy wants to leave you in misery and prevent you from standing for the house. He can't stop what God has already set in motion. But he can make you walk away from it for a time.

Remind yourself that it took a long time to get to this point. You went through a lot of heartache, a lot of hurt, and a lot of disappointment. Just decide that you can't walk away now. You put too much time into moving forward that you just can't give up. Learn to maintain your profession, then learn to manipulate your perspective.

Next, we're going to deal with mastering the process. The process of standing for the house' involves three things. First comes maintenance of your profession, then manipulating your perspective, and then mastering the process. You can get a handle on it if it's important to you.

chapter 6

MASTERING THE PROCESS

The difficulty surrounding the process often proves to be frustrating for the individual caught in the midst. It has been stated in previous chapters that we live in a day and time that is not fond of anything that does not produce immediate results. There are many who choose to forfeit quality for the sake of expediency. The fast-food industry has staked their claim on this concept. No fast-food restaurant can beat good home cooking. Nevertheless, millions of dollars are made by fast-food establishments because they, while inferior to grandma's cooking, can get it done faster.

This prevailing mindset has not limited itself to fast food alone, but it has been adopted by many industries and arenas. It has even impacted the manner in which we seek and believe God. We expect Him to do everything right now. Therefore, it is necessary that believers have their understanding broadened to include God's process in conjunction with the sudden supernatural move of God. God is able to move in an instant and completely turn one's situation around. However, He often uses processes for one's development amidst their deliverance.

When taking a stand for your house, family, or whatever may be the target of your prayers, you will always undergo a process. Maintaining your profession is necessary because when you step out on faith you can not waver, according to James 1:6-7 which reads, "But let him ask in faith, nothing wavering. For he that wavereth is like a wave of the sea driven with the wind and tossed. For let not that man think that he shall receive anything of the Lord." Wavering cancels the request.

> *God is able to move in an instant and completely turn one's situation around. However, He often uses processes for one's development amidst their deliverance.*

Manipulating your perspective provides continued hope as well as peace. Hope operates in partnership with faith. "Now faith is the substance of things hoped for, the evidence of things not seen"

(Hebrews 11:1). Hope provides direction and an assignment for faith to fulfill. So, it is essential to keep hoping if you intend to stay in faith. A hopeful perspective will provide stability and anchor for the soul. Both of these steps, discussed in previous chapters, are important and needed. They target the spiritual nature in you. However, there is another nature that questions and gets frustrated. That nature is the flesh. This final step will equip you to manage the frustration that will come as you strive to master the process.

Hebrews 10:36 provides clarity and context regarding the understanding of what is meant by "the process." It reads, "For ye have need of patience that, after ye have done the will of God, ye might receive the promise." The implication here is that there is some time that passes between doing the will of God and receiving the blessing associated with it. The apostle Paul also echoes this concept in Galatians 6:9 which reads, "And let us not be weary in well doing: for in due season we shall reap, if we faint not." Paul basically says you have to keep doing what is good even though you may not see the immediate benefits from it. However, if you keep going, it will come to pass. Both of these scriptures acknowledge that there is time that elapses between seed time and harvest, completion and manifestation, or faith and fruition. No matter how you choose to phrase it you will have to deal with delay.

It is a common occurrence for the believer to consider any outcome or process that fit within the scope of their desired experience to be the devil. The problem with this line of thinking is the fact that all delay is not demonic. While we know that all things are working together for our good, according to Romans 8:28, the origin of the delay will determine what you may experience during the process. When it comes to the origin of a delay, it can either come from the Lord or the enemy.

There is time that elapses between seed time and harvest, completion and manifestation, or faith and fruition. No matter how you choose to phrase it you will have to deal with delay.

The enemy brings about delay to try and take something from you. An example of this can be seen in Daniel 10:12-13. It reads,

> "Then said he unto me, Fear not, Daniel: for from the first day that thou didst set thine heart to understand, and to chasten thyself before thy God, thy words were heard, and I am come for thy words. But the prince of the kingdom of Persia withstood me one and twenty days: but, lo, Michael one of the chief princes, came to help me; and I remained there with the kings of Persia."

The enemy held up Daniel's prayer to discourage him as well as hinder him from understanding the vision that God had given him. The enemy comes to steal, kill, and destroy. When he sends delay, it is designed to steal something from you.

The other end of the spectrum, as it pertains to delay, is seen with the origin of the delay being the Lord. Just as day is opposite from night the purpose of the enemy is the opposite of the Lord's intention. John 10:10 says, "The thief cometh not, but for to steal, and to kill, and to destroy: I am come that they might have life, and that they might have it more abundantly." If the enemy sends delay to take something from you then the Lord delays in an effort to get something to you.

This can be clearly seen in how Jesus dealt with the sickness of Lazarus in John 11. Verse 6 says, "When he had heard therefore that he was sick, he abode two days still in the same place where he was." This verse seems strange. It said that when Jesus heard that his friend was sick that he stayed where He was. Jesus delayed going to Lazarus. Upon reading the remaining verses it is clear that Lazarus died. Jesus' delay seemingly made the situation worse. However, when it is understood that any delay that is originated by Jesus is designed to get something to you, the plan can be seen unfolding in the text. Verses 14-15 read, "Then said Jesus unto them plainly, Lazarus is dead. And I am glad for your sakes that I was not there, to the intent ye may believe; nevertheless let us go unto him." It is clear that Jesus was trying to get something to the disciples. He was trying to increase their faith.

The enemy delays to take from you while God delays to give to you. Therefore, we must be careful not to call the work of the Lord a trick of the enemy. It may be best not to attempt to categorize it at all until we know for sure. Regardless of its origin, the difficulty in dealing with delay is a real struggle that must be overcome.

> *If the enemy sends delay to take something from you then the Lord delays in an effort to get something to you.*

There are several challenges associated with dealing with delay. One such challenge is in overcoming the pain that is felt when one has to wait. The word of God refers to this pain as a sickness in the book of Proverbs 13:12. It reads, "Hope deferred maketh the heart sick: but when the desire cometh, it is a tree of life." This sick feeling is a reality that must be managed as opposed to being ignored. The key to finding victory in this situation is found within the scripture. The focus must be placed on the word "deferred" and not on "sick." When the attention is placed on "deferred," any pain, fear or discomfort associated with the delay can be endured. In most instances, the key to enduring any season of discomfort is in realizing that it is temporary. At times the delay may feel as though it will never end, however deferred means that the pain is seasonal.

The apostle Paul speaks of this season of temporary struggle in 2 Corinthians 4:17-18. It reads, "For our light affliction, which is but for a moment, worketh for us a far more exceeding and eternal weight of glory; While we look not at the things which are seen, but at the things which are not seen: for the things which are seen are temporal; but the things which are not seen are eternal." Paul not only speaks to the temporal or seasonal aspect of the trial but he urges the believer to focus on the eternal. This is a challenge to change your perspective.

It is important to remember, while dealing with delay, that perspective makes a big difference. Perspective fuels the faith and disposition of a believer. As a matter of fact, Paul tells the church at Philippi that their perspective or the focal point of their thoughts will greatly impact their actions.

> "Finally, brethren, whatsoever things are true, whatsoever things are honest, whatsoever things are just, whatsoever things are pure, whatsoever things are lovely, whatsoever things are of good report; if there be any virtue, and if there be any praise, think on these things" (Philippians 4:8).

Thinking on the good, lovely, just, and honest things aid in combating the sickness that comes with delay. Shifting your focus or altering your perspective prevents discouragement from taking root.

Discouragement is the act of depriving one of courage, hope, or confidence. In other words, it means to dishearten. While you are enduring the process, you must master thought management. Losing hope is not an option. Thoughts of discouragement must be cast out of your mind.

In Paul's second letter to the church at Corinth, he teaches them about spiritual warfare. In particular, the importance of dealing with ungodly thoughts. He says,

> "For though we walk in the flesh, we do not war after the flesh: (For the weapons of our warfare are not carnal, but mighty through God to the pulling down of strong holds;) Casting down imaginations, and every high thing that exalteth itself against the knowledge of God, and bringing into captivity every thought to the obedience of Christ;" (2 Corinthians 10:3-5).

In many cases, the presumption is that all of the hindrances, obstacles, and opposition are external. However, the most difficult things to overcome reside within the mind. The quest to master the process is an ongoing battle to stay in faith and continuously remind oneself that the victory is won, but the process must be endured.

Just as Joshua stood before all of Israel and declared that he and his family would serve the Lord, the believer must also be willing to stand and declare the same. We must stand before our peers, society, and an ever-changing world and acknowledge that our families will not bend to environmental pressures. It is imperative that we instill in our children a since of godly identity and purpose. The promises of God belong to those of us who are His children. Therefore, we must fight to possess and maintain our God given inheritance.

ABOUT THE AUTHOR

Bishop Clarence V. Russell III has been fulfilling the call to preach the Gospel and fulfill a mandate to bring healing and hope to people across the country. His focus has been centered on developing parishioners and proselytes at St. Paul Baptist Church, Suffolk, Virginia.

A graduate of Chowan University, Bishop Russell has earned a Bachelor of Science degree in Religion. He was voted onto the Chowan University Board of Ministers. He is also a Harris Scholar that has studied abroad in England.

After being baptized by his grandfather at an early age and growing up under the leadership of his father, Russell III heard a call from the Lord and at the age of 18 preached his initial sermon. Two years later, he was appointed as the Assistant Pastor of the Mount Carmel Baptist Church with a congregation of just over 2,000 people. He helped revamp and build the youth department.

In November 2000, Bishop Russell, III was called to be the Pastor of St. Paul Baptist Church, Suffolk, Virginia. He has been diligently working for the fulfillment of the vision for this ministry that will help to heal, deliver, and set the captives free.

He has a great love for God and His people. The five-fold assignment for the church is Healing, Economic Empowerment, Authentic Worship, Lifestyle Transitioning, and Serving the Community. Simply put, St. Paul H.E.A.L.S.

Bishop has founded several ministries while leading the people of St. Paul. He mentors young elementary school boys in the Suffolk Public School System and his church has been named Partner of the Year by the Suffolk Public School system for its work.He also serves on the Suffolk Public Schools Superintendent's Key Communicators Network. In an effort to become active in his community, Bishop Russell has attended the Suffolk Neighborhood College. In 2012, Bishop Russell published his first book entitled *Transitioning Into Kingdom Living*.

He is married to Elder Jaimi Brown Russell and they have four children.

www.ingramcontent.com/pod-product-compliance
Lightning Source LLC
Chambersburg PA
CBHW070119110526
44587CB00015BA/2498